LAKE DISTRICT WILD CAMPING

51 GREAT PLACES TO PITCH YOUR TENT IN THE MOUNTAINS

BY RUSS MOORHOUSE

DISTRIBUTED IN THE UK BY AMOUNTAINBIVVY PUBLISHING

INDEX

PAGE

42 – WETHER HILL
43 – MIDDLE FELL
44 – HIGH SPY
46 – WHITE SIDE
47 – GLENRIDDING DODD
49 – THORNTHWAITE CRAG
50 – BLEA RIGG
51 – SEAT SANDLE
53 – RANNERDALE KNOTSS
54 – FLEETWITH PIKE
55 – COLD PIKE
56 – BLACK SAILS
58 - RAISE
59 – HERON PIKE
60 - BIRKS
62 – KNOTT RIGG
63 - WANDHOPE
64 – HIGH PIKE
65 – HIGH TOVE
67 – HIGH RAISE
68 - WETHERLAM
70 – SCAR CRAGS
71 – BLEABERRY FELL
73 – DALE HEAD
75 - GRASMOOR

LIFE IS NOT ABOUT WAITING FOR THE STORM TO PASS
IT'S ABOUT LEARNING TO CAMP IN THE RAIN

Naturehike

ONE OF THE BEST WAYS TO AVOID OTHER PEOPLE IS TO SPEND A NIGHT ON THE MOUNTAINS

SLEEPING ON A MOUNTAIN ALLOWS YOU TO REWILD YOUR SPIRIT

- IT GIVES YOU BACK YOUR CONNECTION WITH THE PLANET

ONE NIGHTS EXPOSURE IN THE MOUNTAINS IS BETTER THAN READING A CARTLOAD OF BOOKS

LOVE FOR THE MOUNTAINS IS NEVER UNREQUITED

Naturehike

ONLY THOSE WHO AWAKE IN A TENT KNOW THE FULL BEAUTY OF REST

THE DARK BLANKET OF THE NIGHT WARMS THE SOUL OF THOSE WHO SLEEP ON THE MOUNTAINS

ONLY AT NIGHT DOES A MOUNTAIN REVEAL IT'S TRUE SELF AND LET ITS WILD SIDE SHOW

AT THE END OF THE DAY YOUR FEET SHOULD BE SMELLY, YOUR HAIR MESSY AND YOUR EYES SPARKLING

THE WILDERNESS HOLDS ANSWERS TO QUESTIONS WE HAVE NOT YET LEARNED TO ASK

WANDERING IS THE BEST WAY TO WALK

I HAVE A DREAM
EVERY NIGHT I SLEEP IN A TENT

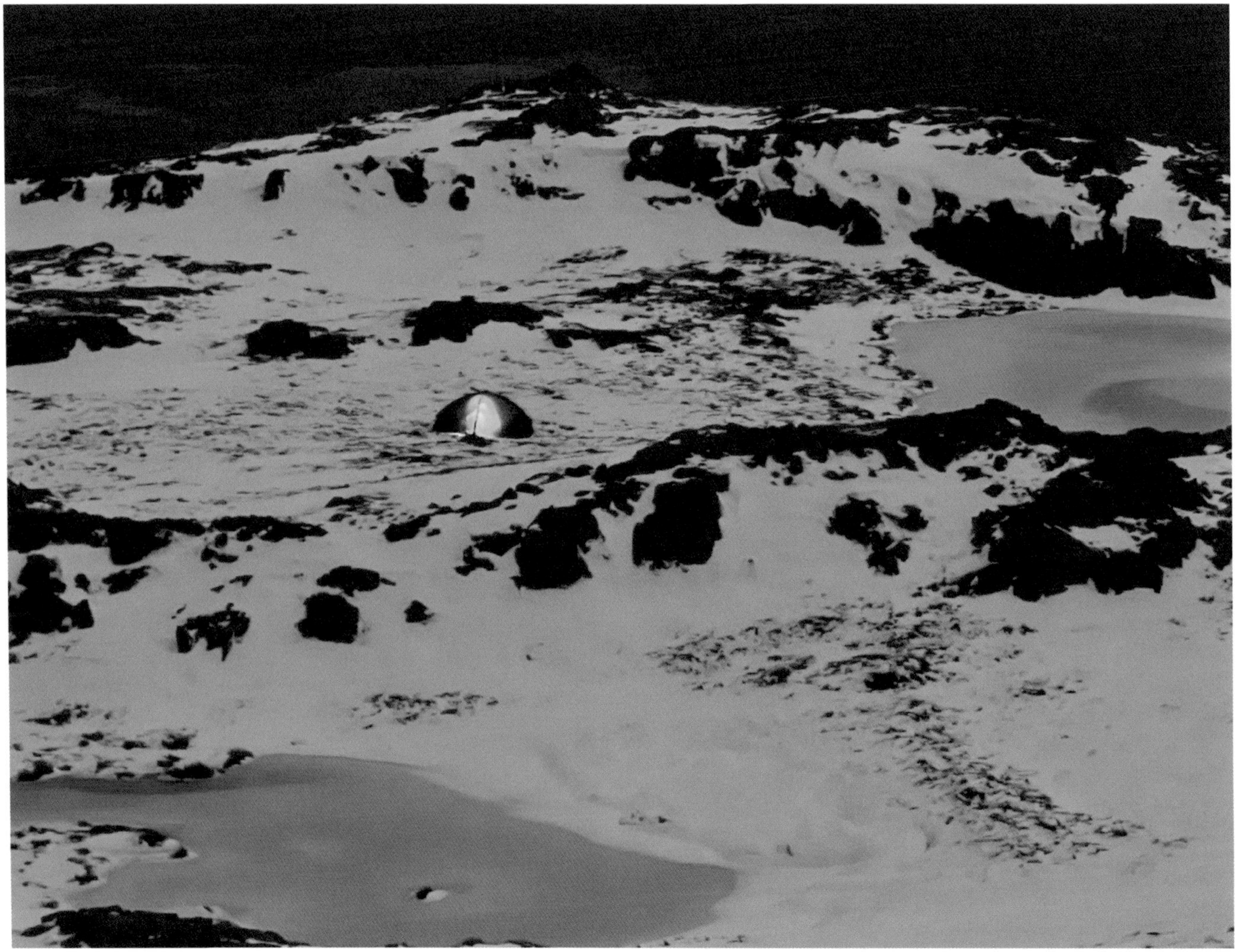

THE WILDERNESS IN OURSELVES IS TAMED BY THE WILDNESS OF THE WILD

LITERALLY A MOUNTAIN IS A LUMP OF ROCK
METAPHORICALLY A MOUNTAIN IS HOME

WE COME TO THE MOUNTAINS TO ESCAPE OTHERS
WE END UP FINDING OURSELVES

THE LESS YOU HAVE
THE MORE YOU GAIN

ONCE YOU HAVE SPENT THE NIGHT ON A MOUNTAIN, YOU WILL FOREVER VIEW IT AS A FRIEND

TO THE MOUNTAINS WE SHALL RETURN

OTHER BOOKS BY RUSS MOORHOUSE

FELL ASLEEP
THE WAINWRONGS

Printed in Great Britain
by Amazon

81962901R00047